My World of Science

MATERIALS

Angela Royston

Heinemann
LIBRARY

H **www.heinemann.co.uk/library**
Visit our website to find out more information about **Heinemann Library** books.

To order:
☎ Phone 44 (0) 1865 888066
🗎 Send a fax to 44 (0) 1865 314091
🖥 Visit the Heinemann Bookshop at www.heinemann.co.uk/library to browse our catalogue and order online.

First published in Great Britain by Heinemann Library, Halley Court, Jordan Hill, Oxford, OX2 8EJ, a division of Reed Educational & Professional Publishing Ltd. Heinemann is a registered trademark of Reed Educational & Professional Publishing Ltd.

OXFORD   MELBOURNE   AUCKLAND   JOHANNESBURG   BLANTYRE
GABORONE   IBADAN   PORTSMOUTH NH (USA)   CHICAGO

Designed by bigtop, Bicester, UK
Originated by Ambassador Litho Ltd.
Printed and bound in Hong Kong/China

05 04 03 02 01
10 9 8 7 6 5 4 3 2 1

ISBN 0 431 13701 3

British Library Cataloguing in Publication Data
Royston, Angela
Materials. – (My world of science)
1. Materials Science – Juvenile literature
I. Title
620.1'1

Acknowledgements
The Publishers would like to thank the following for permission to reproduce photographs:
Corbis: p28; Hutchinson Library: p22; Paul Felix: p16; Photodisc: p27; Robert Harding: pp8, 21, GM Wilkins p18; Sally Greenhill: p14; Science Photo Library: Astrid and Hanns-Frieder Michler p29, Wayne Lawler p26, R Maisonneuve p10; Spectrum Colour Library: p24; Stone: p23; Trevor Clifford: pp4, 6, 7, 11, 17, 19, 25; Trip: P Mitchell p13, N Price p15, N Rogers pp9, 12, D Saunders p20; Unknown: p5.

Cover photograph reproduced with permission of Images.

Every effort has been made to contact copyright holders of any material reproduced in this book. Any omissions will be rectified in subsequent printings if notice is given to the Publisher.

Contents

Any words appearing in the text in bold, **like this**,
are explained in the Glossary.

What are materials?

The word 'material' is often used to mean cloth. But scientists use the word 'material' to mean anything that things are made of.

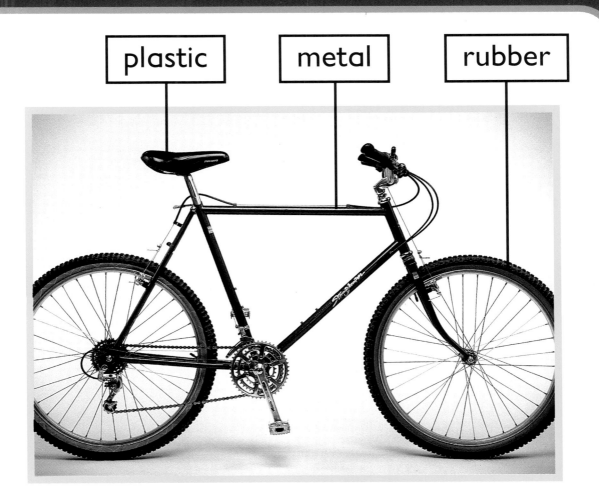

plastic   metal   rubber

This bicycle is made of more than one material. Some things are made mostly of just one material. This book is made mostly of paper.

Where do materials come from?

Materials are either **natural** or **synthetic**. Natural materials come from plants or animals, or are found in the ground. Everything in the picture is a natural material.

Synthetic materials are made from oil by people. Plastic and nylon are two kinds of synthetic material. Some synthetic materials can look like natural ones.

Wood

Wood is a **natural** material. It comes from trees. Some trees are grown specially to be cut down. They are used to make many different things.

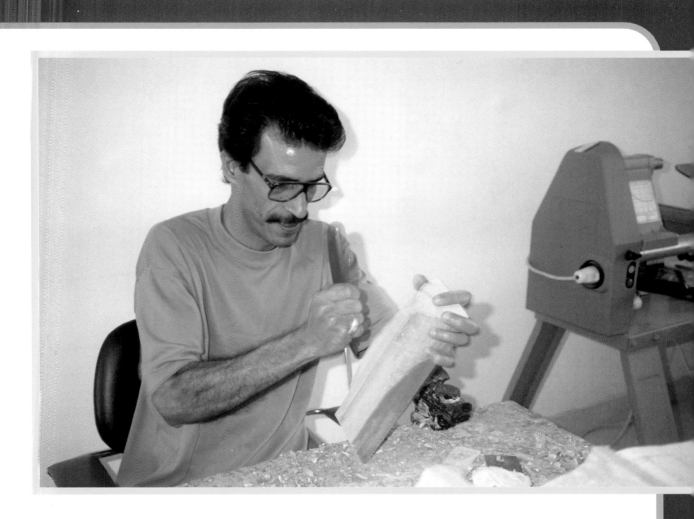

It is easy to cut wood into different shapes. Wood is strong, and it is not as heavy as stone and many metals.

Paper

To make paper, wood is cut into very small pieces. It is then mashed with water to make a pulp. This is spread into a thin layer. When it dries, it becomes sheets of paper.

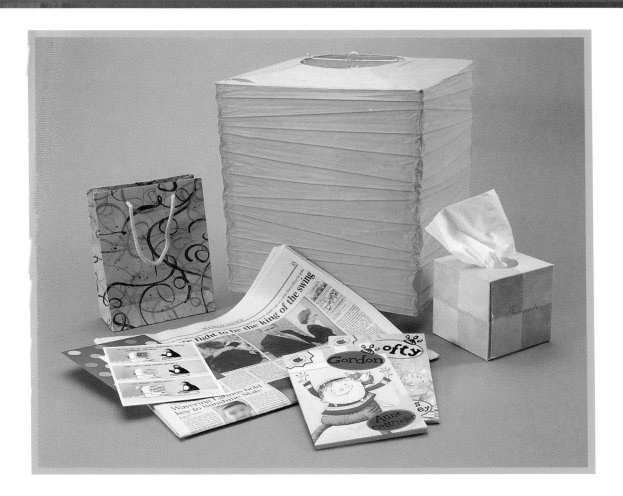

Paper is used for many things. You can write on paper and colour it with ink or paint. Paper is folded to make books, magazines and bags.

Materials from animals

Sheep have thick woolly coats. The wool is shaved off and **spun** into balls of wool. This woman is spinning. Her hat has been **knitted** from wool.

When cows have died, their skin can be made into leather. This pony's saddle and bridle are made of leather.

Rock and stone

Rocks and stones are strong and hard. They are used to build houses and other things. This house is made of stone and so is the roof.

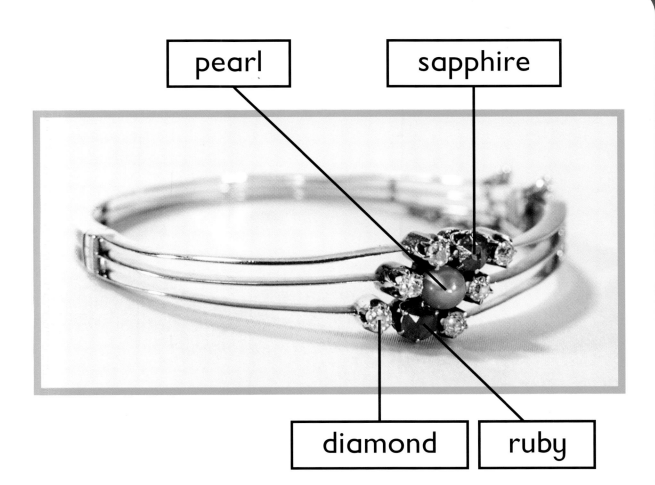

pearl

sapphire

diamond

ruby

Some stones are valuable because they are **rare** and very pretty. When they are **polished**, they sparkle. Sapphires are blue. What colour are rubies?

Clay

Clay is a kind of mud. When it is soft, you can make it into any shape. Then it is baked hard and dried in a hot oven called a kiln.

Bricks and china are made from clay. All of these things are made of brick or china. China breaks easily. What has broken in the picture?

Glass

Glass is made mainly from sand. The sand is heated in a very hot fire until it melts. This man is blowing the **molten** glass into shape.

Some glass is coloured but most glass is transparent. This means you can see through it. Be careful! Glass breaks easily into sharp pieces.

Metals

Metals are found in rocks in the ground. This gold miner is breaking up rock that has gold in it. Gold and silver are **precious** metals.

Most metals are hard, shiny and strong. Iron and aluminium are two metals that are used to make machines. This aeroplane is made of aluminium.

Paint protects

Unless it is protected, iron slowly rusts. It turns brown and crumbles. And wood slowly **rots** if it is left outside in the damp air.

Iron and wood are often covered with
paint to stop them rusting and rotting.
The paint on this ship keeps the water,
rain and damp air out.

Plastic

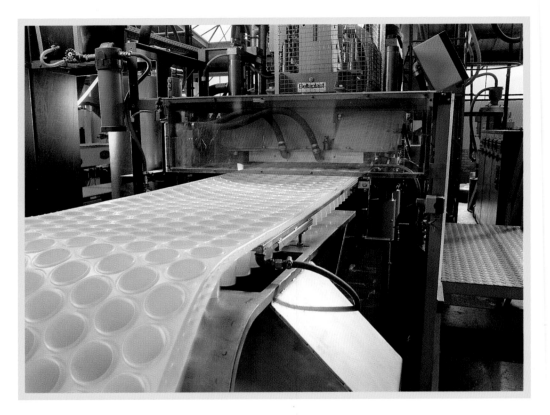

Plastic is made in a factory. Hot, runny plastic is poured into **moulds** to make any kind of shape. Plastic is cheap, light and **waterproof**.

Plastic is used to make many different things. Some plastic is hard, but other plastic can be bent or folded. Which of these plastic things can be folded?

Clothes

Synthetic material is often mixed with **natural** material to make it stronger. Cotton comes from a plant. Polyester, rayon and nylon are made from oil.

Many clothes are made from cotton and polyester. Look at the labels inside your clothes to see what materials they are made of.

Recycling

Materials cost money to make. Some **natural** materials can be **recycled** and used again. Which materials go in this recycling bin?

Most plastic cannot be recycled.
Throwing plastic things away causes
problems because plastic does not **rot**
or rust. Plastic rubbish lasts for ever!

Glossary

knitted threads looped together to make a cloth

molten melted

mould shape that can be filled with liquid. When the liquid hardens it makes the same shape as the mould.

natural materials that come from plants or animals, or are found in the ground

polished rubbed in order to make shiny

precious very valuable

rare not very common

recycle to use again

rot become weak and crumbly

spun twisted into a long thread

synthetic made from oil by people

waterproof keeps water out

Answers

Page 15 – Rock and stone
Rubies are red.

Page 17 – Clay
A mug has broken.

Page 25 – Plastic
The plastic bag can be folded. The straps of the sandals, the green file and the drinking straw can probably be folded too.

Page 28 – Recycling
Metal cans go in the recycling bin.

Index